FROM CONTRACTOR TO CONSUMER:

the Truth about Heating, Air Conditioning, and Home
Comfort Systems

FROM CONTRACTOR TO CONSUMER:

the Truth about Heating, Air Conditioning, and Home Comfort Systems

What Your Contractor Won't Tell you

Joe Gorman

iUniverse, Inc.
New York   Bloomington

From Contractor to Consumer:
the Truth about Heating, Air Conditioning, and Home Comfort Systems
What Your Contractor Won't Tell you

Copyright © 2009 Joe Gorman

iUniverse books may be ordered through booksellers or by contacting:

iUniverse
1663 Liberty Drive
Bloomington, IN 47403
www.iuniverse.com
1-800-Authors (1-800-288-4677)

ISBN: 978-1-4401-7817-7 (pbk)
ISBN: 978-1-4401-7818-4 (ebk)

Printed in the United States of America

iUniverse rev. date: 12/3/2009

Contents

Acknowledgments

I would like to thank the following people.

First, my father and mother, for sharing knowledge, pushing me, and teaching me how to be the best at whatever I choose to do.

Second, Earl Flint of CFM Equipment in Sacramento, California, for believing in his clientele, bringing an industry together through the creation of the CFM Equipment Alliance, and providing avenues to better learning in the home comfort, indoor air quality, and heating and air conditioning industries. Without the avenues he provided, I might not have found my true career passion and or developed into the performance contractor and consultant I am today.

Third, I would like to thank the following individuals for their dedication and commitment to the continued education and training of all the professionals in the home comfort, indoor air quality, building performance, and heating and air conditioning industries who are willing to listen and perform.

Rob Faulke, Dominic Guarino, Jim Davis, and all my friends at the National Comfort Institute, Sheffield Lake, Ohio

Rick Chitwood of Chitwood Energy Management, Shasta, California

Al D'Ambola of D'Ambola Associates, Avon Lake, Ohio

Finally, most importantly, I thank my wonderful wife Tricia and three daughters. They all love me, stand behind all that I do, and put up with me. Without them, I would not be the man I am today.

About the Author

Home comfort and the expertise that creates it are definitely in Joe Gorman's family. Mr. Gorman has worked in the electrical and HVAC industries since childhood, helping his grandfather and father in their contracting businesses and learning about electricity, heating, and air conditioning.

After receiving his bachelor's degree from San Jose State University in business administration and accounting, Mr. Gorman earned an associate's degree in refrigeration and air conditioning technology from San Jose City College. Soon thereafter, he started JP Gorman Inc. to serve business and residential electrical, heating, and air conditioning needs in California's Santa Clara Valley. Then, realizing that his true passion lay in the field of home comfort, he developed expertise in airflow and combustion analysis. His National Comfort Institute (NCI) certifications in air diagnostics, residential air balancing, light commercial air balancing, combustion analysis, and carbon monoxide analysis provided his expertise in his passions—the design and installation of highly efficient, balanced, and safe home comfort systems, indoor air quality systems and the performance testing of light commercial and residential comfort systems. Having sold the assets of his contracting business in Silicon Valley, Joe Gorman now resides and operates J P Gorman Inc. dba High Performance Energy Solutions in the Sacramento area with his wonderful wife and children. He continues to pursue his dream of making Northern California comfort systems safer, more efficient, and more comfortable for the people who own them. Currently, Joe Gorman is the only NCI-certified Carbon Monoxide and Combustion Analyst in Northern California outside of San Jose.

Introduction

Very often, I find myself sitting across a kitchen table from clients who want to purchase a new home comfort system. Also very often, I can tell that the people making the purchasing decision do not understand the concepts and terms I use. Nor do they understand the complex interactions of heating, air conditioning, and home comfort systems. I decided to write this book to educate consumers about heating, air conditioning, and home comfort systems, how they work, and how to purchase one.

After all, in my twenty-six years in the HVAC industry, I have only seen books and seminars intended to *sell* heating, air conditioning, and home comfort systems to homeowners! This guidebook is the first I have seen to educate homeowners on these systems and help them make informed purchasing and installation decisions. My information comes from my years of continuing professional education, sales, design, and installation of thousands of furnaces and air conditioning systems, also known as HVAC systems. My knowledge also stems from my hands-on performance testing of many comfort systems for home and business owners.

As we begin this exploration, you should know that **all furnaces and air conditioners do the same things. They heat or cool your home.** Despite the many opinions on different manufacturers, the brand name of the equipment has little influence on how comfortably and efficiently they perform these functions. You and the heating and air conditioning professional you choose control those results. In fact, many of the manufacturers use the same parts, manufactured by the same companies, in their products. No such product is guaranteed to work perfectly when taken home and simply installed to take the place of another. A heating/air conditioning system of any brand must be installed by an individual with many years of training and education. When a system is properly sized and installed, it will give you many years of problem-free enjoyment, and the contractor who performs that installation makes the difference between optimal or unsatisfactory results.

Almost anybody can put the pieces of a heating a cooling system together, and many people *think* they know what they are doing because they can. However, the key word here is *think*. What happens after you put it together? All home comfort systems require on-site assembly; in a best-case scenario, they are fine-tuned to work properly and efficiently after assembly. That is why you should purchase only equipment suitable for your needs, only from a professional with whom you can work comfortably, and only from a company that will do the best job for you.

This book is written so that it is easy to understand, with the intent of avoiding excessive detail and technical jargon. I created it to educate you on heating and cooling system operation, on how the equipment and duct systems work together, and on how to purchase a home comfort system. It will also help you choose the right contractor for the system installation in your home or business and give you key points to be aware of before, during, and after the installation.

Whether you are a homeowner preparing to make this important purchase decision for your home, a beginner just getting into the heating and air conditioning industry, or a seasoned professional, the intent of this book is to guide and educate you on the following topics;

- heating, air conditioning and home comfort system operation
- the decision process for choosing and buying the appropriate system
- the decision process for choosing the right contractor for the job

As a homeowner, you will be informed and ready in preparation for choosing and meeting with HVAC contractors during your purchase. As a trainee entering the industry or even a seasoned professional, you will learn additional improvements for your sales strategies, additional information on HVAC systems, and some new ideas. Use this book as a guide to increase the value of your installation practices, the quality of your installations, your knowledge of comfort systems, and the impact of your customer service practices. I hope you will keep this book as a guide to teach those who work with you as well as the homeowners you serve on a daily basis.

Chapter 1
The Home Comfort System

Furnace and air conditioning systems, also known as home comfort systems, are probably the most expensive and important appliances that will be purchased and installed in your home. These systems affect the comfort and safety of the home's occupants. When you decide whether you actually love your home, comfort can be the deciding factor—and a poorly designed, poorly installed, or improperly sized furnace and air conditioning system will make you uncomfortable! It will also drain your bank account. A faulty comfort system may be costing you unnecessary outlay on utility bills as you read this book... you may have been paying out too much cash for too little comfort for years.

How much? Heating and cooling costs generally make up 40 to 50% of your total utility bill each year. By replacing your inefficient system and repairing any duct system design and installation flaws now, you can cut your utility bill by 30% or more, not to mention saving money on expensive repairs and avoiding the inconvenience of untimely breakdowns. Just think—the savings on your utility bill and the savings on expensive repairs will actually help you pay for the new system or the renovation of your existing system.

A poorly designed, incorrectly installed, and improperly sized furnace and air conditioning system can affect your health, causing sickness, serious injury, or even death. Such systems can also cause damage to homes. How would you like to purchase a new furnace for thousands of dollars and then watch you house burn to the ground? That happens.

Don't let it happen to you.

A properly trained and educated professional should always perform a furnace and air conditioning system installation. Such professionals are hard to find.

Over the years, big-box retailers, some unscrupulous contractors, and even some manufacturers and distributors have tried to commodify HVAC systems, and that is just wrong. By *commodify*, I mean that they want you to think you can buy a home comfort system just as if you were buying a refrigerator. They want you to believe that you can just take it home, uncrate it, put the parts together, and plug it in.

This is NOT true.

It just can't happen.

It is impossible, no matter what anybody tells you.

In a sense, these retailers and contractors, who apparently really do not understand airflow or system performance, have succeeded in making customers think their products are plug-and-play. It is an all too common misconception that furnaces and air conditioners can be simply bought, put together, and plugged in, and they will work perfectly and operate at the efficiency rated on the box when the system was purchased. This just isn't going to happen.

A furnace and an air conditioner do not make up a home comfort system; they are just parts of one. A home comfort system is made up of many different parts and has many different systems: heating, cooling, electrical, filtration, control, exhaust, and ducting. The very important ducting system is the least understood and most frequently overlooked component. All these systems need to be properly matched, sized, and installed to work as one complete, safe and efficient home comfort system.

Just because you purchase an Energy Star, or high efficiency-rated furnace, 90% or above, and an Energy Star-rated high SEER air conditioner, 14 SEER or above, does not mean that the system will operate efficiently, comfortably, or safely. Sizing is the issue. Again, I cannot stress this point enough—furnaces, air conditioners, and duct systems should be sized properly for your home. Sizing by the square footage of the house, which is what most companies do, just does not work. Many contractors do not know how to size the system for your home properly, and others are just too lazy.

The only way to size the equipment properly is to perform a complete load calculation. Demand one!

I must emphasize this point, and I will say it again.

All the above systems need to be sized and installed properly to operate and perform efficiently.

All the above systems need to be sized and installed properly to keep you, your family, and your home safe.

All the above systems need to be sized and installed properly to keep you, your family, and your home comfortable.

To assure this efficiency, safety, and comfort, the above systems need to be sized and installed properly by a professional.

When I say professional, I do not mean someone with just a contractors license. Look for a licensed HVAC contractor with additional certifications from organizations like the National Comfort Institute(NCI) or National Balancing Institute(NBI). Certifications provided by organizations like these prove that you are working with a true professional who has the dedication and understanding of the components of building and system performance.

Chapter 2
The Load Calculation

The lack of load calculations is the number one reason that furnaces, air conditioners, and duct systems are not sized correctly. Too many contractors DO NOT perform load calculations. Sizing an air conditioner by square footage or replacing an old one with a new one of the same size just does not work.

A load calculation is the only right way to size a furnace, air conditioner, and duct system, a home comfort system, for your home. A load calculation should be performed on every single furnace, air conditioner, duct system, and home comfort system replacement. NO EXCEPTIONS!

A load calculation is very complicated. However, thanks to computers, they have become much easier. There is absolutely no reason not to perform one except ignorance.

When performing a load calculation, many different aspects and features of the home are taken into consideration. Solar orientation, window size, window R-value, shading, wall, floor and ceiling insulation, doors, building materials, type of foundation, type of roof, ceiling height, type of floors, square footage of the home, type of ductwork, and many other considerations of how your home has been constructed are needed to perform the load calculation. Since there are so many different types of climates and humidity levels in the USA that effect system performance requirements and comfort, even the area of the country where you live is taken into consideration Therefore, you can see that a contractor must know much more than your home's square footage to size your furnace, air conditioner, and duct system properly.

According to the National Comfort Institute, the national average of furnace and air conditioning performance is just 57%.

57%.

That's it!

This means that just over half of the heating and cooling that your home comfort system produces is getting into the conditioned area of your home. So you are paying almost twice, if not more, what you should be paying to heat and cool your home! This would not be so bad except that the largest portion of your utility bill each month goes towards heating and cooling your home. Would you buy a car that only achieved 57% of the gas mileage it was rated to get? Most likely not, and you must own a dividend-paying stock in your utility company if you want to pay an almost-double utility bill. Why else would you tolerate a home comfort system that only operates at 57% of its rating and pay twice what you should be paying each month to your utility company?

> The National Comfort Institute has tested and balanced over 50,000 homes and businesses nationwide. It has proven documentation that the average performance of installed heating and air conditioning systems nationwide is 57%. The NCI also provides certification training and courses in air balancing, air diagnostics, carbon monoxide analysis, and combustion analysis.

A properly sized duct system, furnace, and air conditioner is the answer to this problematic issue of fuel waste and monetary waste, crucial for obtaining the name-tag efficiency rating of the furnace and air conditioner you purchase. Whether you replace the complete duct system or renovate your existing duct system when changing out your furnace and air conditioner, proper sizing is worthwhile.

Demand a load calculation!

Chapter 3
The Heating System

Heat always goes to cold. This is the Second Law of Thermodynamics. When you set the thermostat to heat the air in your home, the furnace actually ADDS heat to the air and everything else in your home. If your favorite chair is colder than the air temperature in your home, your chair will keep on absorbing the heat from the air until it is the same temperature. The same goes for the walls, the carpets, the sheetrock, the two-by-fours in the walls, the drapes over your windows, and every other item in your house. They all absorb heat at different rates when they are colder than their surroundings, and they all give off heat at different rates when warmer than their surroundings. Think about what you notice when you take a hot meal out of the oven. The food gives off heat and its wonderful smell of goodness, but only until its temperature matches the room temperature. And the opposite happens when you remove ice cream from the freezer. The ice cream absorbs heat from the warmer environment and melts. Everything absorbs and gives off heat at different rates. This is why a furnace will run longer on some days and a shorter time on others. The colder it is in your home, the colder the items in your home are, so the longer it takes to warm it all up. You are not just warming the air in your home; you are transferring heat and warming everything.

FURNACE OPERATION

Each time the thermostat is set to warm the house, the air in your home is circulated by the furnace blower and distributed by the duct system. As the cold air passes through the furnace, a little more heat is added to the air every time the air passes through the heat exchanger within the furnace until the thermostat is satisfied and tells the furnace to shut off. The colder it is in the home, the longer a furnace will run. Each time the warm air passes an item that is colder than the air, the item absorbs some heat from the air and gradually warms up. And the opposite happens after the furnace turns off. As the air in your home cools off, the warm furniture, floors, walls and other items in your home radiate, or give some heat back, to the air. This process helps maintain a steady temperature in your home.

It is imperative, both for your wallet and for your comfort, to make sure that the furnace in your home is not too small and not too large. It is extremely important to have your heating contractor perform a complete load calculation on your home _before_ a furnace is chosen to be installed in your home.

The goal of heating your home is to maintain a steady, comfortable temperature. The only way to obtain this goal is to heat everything in your home.

Why can't an inaccurately sized furnace do this? A furnace that is too small for your home will run continuously, never heat the home or its contents, and cost you an arm and a leg each month in gas and electricity. The small furnace will not produce enough heat to warm the house or its contents, so the thermostat will never be satisfied, and it will never tell the furnace to turn off.

A furnace that is too large, the most common problem in my experience, will provide too much sensible heat to your home. Sensible heat is the heat that you sense or feel. Too much sensible heat will cause the air in your home to heat up really fast and cause the thermostat to be satisfied too soon, which turns the furnace off. When a furnace adds too much sensible heat to the air, the air heats up fast and does not allow your home's structure or contents to absorb the heat carried in the air.

The thermostat only senses the air temperature where it is located, and that's it. Therefore, since the thermostat has the false impression that everything in your home is warmed up when only the air is warm, the thermostat tells the furnace to shut off. The furnace will then turn on again and off again very rapidly and very often until all the contents in your home have warmed up, wasting gas and electricity every time it does so. This action is known as cycling. Up to ten times more energy is used every time your furnace starts up in this way, as compared to continuous operation, so you want to avoid rapid cycling.

Adding too much heat to the air with an oversized furnace is also one of the reasons that you or someone in your house keeps running back and forth to the thermostat to turn it down and then up over and over. You are uncomfortable! You're overheating fast, then freezing! Then overheating! Then freezing yet again! Get the picture? If you are having this experience in your home, your furnace is oversized or your duct system is unbalanced—or, most likely, both problems exist.

Remember, everything in your home absorbs and gives off heat at a different rate or speed. When the furnace turns off and the air temperature starts to cool down, the warm contents of your home start to give off some of the heat they earlier absorbed, warming the cooler air. This effect is called radiant heat. When the radiant heat coming off the contents of your home can no longer keep the air warm, the air temperature drops below the thermostat setting. Then the furnace will turn on to warm everything up again. This cycle repeats itself as your system tries to keep you comfortable.

In contrast, when you have a properly sized furnace installed and allow it to cycle as it should and run for a period of time, the furnace will heat up all the contents of your home and the structure itself. Your furnace will run less, and you, your family, and your home will be more comfortable. Because you have a properly sized furnace, all the contents in your home will absorb and give off heat all day and night to assist the furnace and the thermostat in keeping your home's sensible temperature at a steady state and you and your family efficiently comfortable.

SETTING THE THERMOSTAT

Set the thermostat to the temperature that keeps you comfortable. On a properly sized furnace, it is better to program and leave the thermostat set for one temperature while you are home and leave it alone. This will allow the thermostat to maintain the temperature in the home in the most efficient and comfortable manner. Sometimes, after you purchase and install a new, properly sized system, it takes a few days to find the most comfortable temperature setting—but then you'll experience pure bliss.

It is okay to have and maintain a lower temperature while you are not home or while you are sleeping to help conserve energy. Remember, though, that the lower the temperature, the longer it will take to heat up the home and its contents, and the more energy you will use to heat the house up.

Chapter 4
Furnaces

Furnaces generate heat. Period.

After a thermostat tells a furnace to turn on, the furnace goes through many safety checks before the gas valve opens and the gas ignites. After the gas ignites and starts to heat the air, the primary circuit board, the brain of the furnace, continually monitors the safety devices for safe operation. Should a problem be detected, the furnace will shut down and go into lockout mode. When a furnace goes into lockout mode, a properly trained service technician should be called for the repair. One way to tell if your furnace is in lockout mode is that your blower continues to run and will not turn off, no matter what you do.

Believe it or not, despite all the different brand names, there are basically just three types of furnaces: single stage, two stage, and variable speed two stage. Furnaces are available now in two different efficiency ratings, mid-efficiency (today's low efficiency), and high efficiency (Energy Star).

The efficiency rating is the annual fuel utilization efficiency (AFUE). Simply stated, the AFUE is how much heat is generated versus how much heat is wasted on an annual basis when heating your home—how much money is being used to heat your home versus how much money is flowing out of the furnace exhaust pipe each time you use your furnace. If you spend $100.00 to heat your home, a properly sized and installed 80% efficient furnace will waste about $20 worth of fuel every time it is used, and a properly sized and installed 96% efficient furnace will only waste about $4 worth of fuel every time it is used. If your furnace is not properly sized or installed, you'll waste money along with the heat that goes out the exhaust pipe, no matter what the efficiency rating of the equipment.

Which furnace would you rather have, and what type of installation do you want?

It's your decision. It's your money.

Again, all furnaces all must be sized properly by performing a complete load calculation. And you must make an informed choice of furnace.

TYPES OF FURNACES

The single stage furnace produces 100% of the output heat it is rated to produce each time it is turned on. All these furnaces contain a multiple speed blower.

The two stage furnace, at first, produces 50% to 60% of the output heat it is rated for, depending on the manufacturer. If needed, this furnace will turn on at full capacity. A two stage furnace contains a multiple speed blower and should always be controlled by a two stage thermostat. Contrary to popular belief, a two stage furnace is _not_ more efficient than a single stage furnace. However, a two stage furnace _may_ provide more comfortable heating than a single stage furnace.

The **variable speed two stage furnace**, at first, produces 50% to 60% of the output heat it is rated for; if needed, it will turn on at full capacity. This two-stage furnace contains a variable speed blower and should always be controlled by a two-stage thermostat. The variable speed blower is the most efficient blower in a furnace and is electrically up to eight times more efficient than a standard multiple speed blower, which is installed in other types of furnaces. With the new 13 SEER standard efficiency rating for air conditioning, I recommend that any furnace you purchase in any efficiency contain a variable speed blower when you buy it along with an air conditioner.

EFFICIENCIES OF FURNACES OPERATING IN TODAY'S HOMES

The 55% to 72% efficient furnace (low efficiency) is the type of standard efficiency furnace used prior to 1990. These furnaces are no longer made. If you have one of these, get rid of it. If your furnace has a pilot that is on all of the time, you have a low efficiency furnace. Get rid of it!

The **80% efficient furnace (mid efficiency)** is the standard efficiency rating used today. Fuel is ignited with a spark igniter or a hot surface igniter.

The 90% efficient furnace and above (high efficiency) is the Energy Star-rated furnace, which is-up to 96% efficient. Fuel is ignited by a hot surface igniter.

Furnace Type	Benefit
single stage furnace	heats home faster
two stage furnace	heats more comfortably than a single stage quieter than a single stage when properly sized
variable speed furnace	quietest furnace available heats home most comfortably most efficient blower motor best furnace to use with indoor air quality products best to use with 13 SEER or greater air conditioners
low efficiency furnace 72% and lower	no benefits no longer manufactured minimal safety controls
80% efficient	more efficient than standard natural draft older models (prior to 1990) one to twenty-year warranty on heat exchanger one to five-year standard parts warranty one manufacturer offers a lifetime furnace replacement on its stainless steel heat exchanger
90% efficient	lifetime warranty on heat exchanger up to ten-year standard part warranty efficiencies up to 96% saves money every time it's used safest furnace available most likely the last furnace you will buy as long as you own your home one manufacturer offers a lifetime furnace replacement on its stainless steel heat exchanger

Chapter 5
The Cooling System

Cooling systems remove heat. Period.

Oh, yes! Cooling! Nothing feels better than a nice cool home on a hundred-degree day. In my humble opinion, air conditioning is the greatest process ever invented. You can always keep adding clothes to stay warm, but there is only so much you can take off!

Air conditioners all operate the same way. They transfer heat. They are made to remove heat from the interior of your home and transfer that heat to the exterior of your home. The cooling system in your home actually works thermally opposite to your heating system and is a little more complicated. I will do my best to keep the explanations simple, but you can always go to a technical college for classes or purchase technical manuals to learn more.

To have air conditioning, you need to add a refrigeration or cooling system to the furnace. The cooling system uses the furnace blower to move air and is made up of three additional components—the evaporator, the line set, and the condenser. These three parts make up the refrigeration system.

The evaporator is bolted onto the furnace, and its purpose is to absorb heat from the air inside of your home and transfer that heat to the refrigerant contained within the refrigeration system. Evaporator size must be matched to the condenser and furnace blower to work properly.

The line set is the copper tubing that connects the evaporator to the condenser, and its purpose is to transfer Freon, the refrigerant gas and liquid, between the evaporator and the condenser. Line sets must be properly sized to transport the right amount of heat and refrigerant.

The condenser is the large box located outside your home. This is the component that people often refer to as "the air conditioner." Its purpose is to transfer heat from the refrigerant gas to the outside air. The condenser must be properly sized to cool your home, and properly matched to the evaporator and furnace blower.

AIR CONDITIONER OPERATION

Some air conditioning systems have safety check features that operate when the thermostat prompts the air conditioner to turn on. With all air conditioning systems, you will hear the furnace blower motor and the condenser outside your home when they start to run.

Rather than adding cold air to your home, the cooling system actually absorbs heat from the air inside your home. Each time the air passes through the evaporator section of the cooling system, heat is absorbed, leaving you with cold air. Each time the furnace blower circulates air through your home through the duct system, the warm return air passes through the evaporator many times. Each time the warm air passes through the evaporator, a little more heat is removed from the air until the air temperature of your home matches that of the thermostat setting. Once the air temperature of the air in your home matches the temperature that you have set on the thermostat, the thermostat becomes satisfied and tells the air conditioner to turn off.

Not only the air is cooled when an air conditioner operates. Heat is also being removed from everything in the house—walls, floors, carpets, drapes, furniture, and anything else within the conditioned space that is hotter than the thermostat setting. The hotter it is in the home, the longer the air conditioner will run.

At the same time that the air is being circulated through your home and duct system, refrigerant is being circulated from the condenser outside your home. The refrigerant goes through the line set and to the evaporator, which is attached to the furnace. The blower in the furnace moves the air through the evaporator coil, where the transfer of heat occurs. Therefore, during the cooling mode, warm air enters the evaporator, and colder air leaves.

The Second Law of Thermodynamics: Heat goes to cold. The refrigeration system contains a chemical known as freon, a low-temperature liquid that has a boiling point of about -40° F. As liquid freon approaches the evaporator, it passes through a metering device that causes a change of pressure inside the refrigerant system and causes the refrigerant to expand rapidly and boil off while changing its state to a gas as it proceeds through the evaporator. Because the refrigerant is boiling off and changing its form to a gaseous liquid at such a low temperature, it absorbs the heat from the air, which is passing by on the outside of the evaporator. This heated refrigerant travels through the large pipe of the line set to the condenser, where the heat is expelled to the cooler outside air.

Remember, heat always goes to cold. In its cooling function, the air conditioner actually *removes* heat from the air, leaving the air cold.

THE AIR COOLING CYCLE

Even though the furnace blower turns on, the gas valve inside of your furnace does not open, so heat is not generated by the furnace. The furnace blower circulates the cool air (supply air), which was cooled by the evaporator, through the duct system to the rooms of your home. After the cool air travels through your house, it warms up by absorbing heat from the contents of your home. Each time the cool air passes an item that is warmer than the air, some of the heat is absorbed from that item into the air, and that item is left in a cooler state. The air, which has traveled through your home, then returns to the duct system as warm air (return air) back to the evaporator, which is attached to the furnace. As the warm return air from the house is pushed through the evaporator, a little more heat is removed from the air every time this air passes until the thermostat is satisfied and tells the furnace blower and air conditioning system to shut off.

THE REFRIGERANT CYCLE

When an air conditioner is running and the furnace blower is circulating the air throughout your home via the duct system, the blower pushes the warm return air from inside your home through the evaporator. As the warm indoor air passes through the evaporator, the heat in the air is absorbed from the air and into the refrigerant. The refrigerant then carries the heat through the larger pipe of the line set, called the suction line, to the condenser outside the house. While the refrigerant travels through the condenser, another fan, called the condenser fan, pulls the cooler outside air through the condenser coil. There the heat is released from the refrigerant to the outside air. Yes, even at a hundred degrees, the outside air is cooler than the refrigerant temperature. The cooled refrigerant then travels back to the evaporator via the small pipe of the line set, called the liquid line, and the process starts all over again.

AIR CONDITIONER SIZING

For both your wallet and your comfort, it is imperative to make sure that the air conditioner in your home is not too small and not too large. This is why it is extremely important to have your air conditioning contractor perform a complete cooling load calculation on your home *before* an air conditioner is chosen and installed. A larger air conditioner will not help you or your comfort; it will ruin it.

A furnace that is too small for your home will run continuously while failing to heat the home or its contents and will cost you an arm and a leg each month in gas and electricity. A too-small air conditioner will not absorb enough heat to cool the home or its contents, so the thermostat will never be satisfied, and it will never tell the air conditioner to turn off. The air conditioner will waste electricity and money every time it turns on.

An air conditioner that is too large, the most common problem in my cooling experience, will provide too much sensible cooling to your home. Sensible cooling is heat that is removed from the air, or the cooling that you feel. Air conditioners also remove moisture from the air, which contains latent heat. It takes longer to absorb latent heat than it does sensible heat, so the latent heat and moisture is not absorbed properly if an air conditioner is too large. This scenario will leave you with a sticky, wet feeling.

Too much sensible cooling—absorption of the heat which you feel—will cause the air in your home to cool down really fast and cause the thermostat to be satisfied too soon, which turns the air conditioner off. Don't forget—the thermostat only senses the air temperature where it is located, and that's it. When the cooling system removes a lot of sensible heat but not enough moisture from the air, the air cools down too fast and does not allow your home's structure or contents to cool down enough. So the thermostat has the false impression that everything in your home has cooled down, even though only the air has cooled. Then the thermostat tells the air conditioner to shut off, the contents and structure of the home release a lot of the heat they are holding, and the air conditioner turns on and off again very rapidly and repeatedly until all the contents of your home and the structure have cooled down, wasting electricity and money every time it operates.

Removing too much sensible heat from the air with an oversized air conditioner is also one of the reasons that people keep running back and forth to the thermostat to turn it up again and down again because they are too cold, and then too hot. With an oversized air conditioner, you are uncomfortable! First you're chilly, then hot! Then freezing! And so the cycle of discomfort repeats itself.

Remember, everything in your home gives absorbs and off heat at a different rate. Therefore, if the sensible heat, latent heat, and moisture are not absorbed from the air and the contents of your home properly, you and others in your home will be uncomfortable.

By installing a properly sized air conditioner, matching it to a properly sized evaporator coil, matching it to a properly sized furnace blower, matching it to a proper sized duct system, and allowing it to run the way it should, for a period of time, you will allow the system to remove moisture and both types of heat from the air, the structure, and the contents of your home. Your air conditioner will run less, and you, your family, and your home will be more comfortable. Because you have a properly sized air conditioner, all the contents in your home will release heat more easily all day and night to assist the air conditioner and the thermostat in keeping your sensible temperature at a steady state, and you and your family comfortable.

With a properly sized air conditioner, it is best to set the thermostat at one temperature while you are home and leave it alone. This will allow the thermostat to maintain the temperature in the home in the most efficient and comfortable manner. It's fine to maintain a higher temperature while sleeping or away from home; however, the warmer the house gets, the longer it will take to cool it and its contents down, and the more electricity the cooling system will consume.

Chapter 6
Air Conditioning Equipment

Residential split system air conditioners come in seven different sizes, 1.5 to 5 tons. A complete load calculation is the only way to determine the proper size air conditioner needed for your home.

Like furnaces, air conditioners are sized by British Thermal Units, or BTUs. A BTU is the measurement of the amount of heat it takes to raise one pound of water one degree Fahrenheit. 12,000 BTUs equal one ton of cooling. The goal of an air conditioner is to remove BTUs from your home. A three-ton air conditioner is required to have 36,000 BTU's (12,000 BTU's x 3 tons) of heat removal. The only real difference between properly sized air conditioners for your home, besides comfort problems, is how efficiently they operate. This value is called the seasonal energy efficiency rating, the SEER. The SEER, simply stated, is how much cooling you will get for your dollar. The higher the SEER, the more cooling you will get for each dollar you spend on electricity and gas.

SEER Rating	Benefit
12 or less	None. These SEER ratings were only available prior to 2006.
13	the new minimum efficiency allowed by law as of January 23, 2006 30% more efficient than a 10 SEER up to 10 year compressor warranty can be very quiet
14	Energy Star rated extremely quiet extremely efficient some brands offer lifetime replacement warranty could be the last air conditioner you will ever purchase for your home
16-19	Energy Star rated extremely quiet extremely efficient some brands offer lifetime replacement warranty could be the last air conditioner you will ever purchase for your home an 18 SEER air conditioner is twice as efficient as a 9 SEER air conditioner (most common in the late 80s to mid 90s)

Chapter 7
The Electrical System

The electrical system is the single most dangerous system you will find in a home, and it is not to be taken lightly. Many times in my career, I have been told that homeowners will do their own electrical work because "the electrical is easy, and my husband will do it so we can save money." My response to this absurd comment is, "Electricity is the only system in your home that can kill you instantly! Do you love your husband and want to keep him around?"

Most say yes, but a few ...

So if you love your husband, your family, and your house, do everyone a favor: *Let a professional work with the electricity.*

Make sure, too, that your professional has an electrical license. After over twenty-five years in the electrical, heating, and air conditioning industries (I was brought up in an electrical contracting family and hold current electrical as well as heating and air conditioning licenses), I still don't know why the building departments allow heating and air conditioning contractors who do not have electrical licenses to do the high-voltage electrical work on equipment installations. Someday the building inspectors will do a more complete job of inspecting the complete electrical installation of the air conditioning equipment and realize that a licensed electrician needs to do this portion of the work.

I will add, though, that because of their problem-solving and controls skills; most really good HVAC service technicians can troubleshoot electrical problems better than a lot of tradespeople who are considered electricians.

ELECTRICITY IN YOUR HOME

The electrical system in your home needs to be large enough to handle the increased load of an air conditioner. There are some general rules of thumb that are followed by contractors and your building inspector concerning the size of your electrical service and the quantity of large electrical appliances your home contains. However, if you are adding air conditioning to a home that did not have it before, an electrical load calculation needs to be performed on your home. This calculation is different from the heating and cooling load calculation we discussed earlier, and it should only be performed by a qualified electrician. Its purpose is to determine if your home also needs an electrical panel upgrade.

Even though electricity is a completely different industry, it is essential that your heating and air conditioning contractor understands electrical theory, knows how to work with electricity safely, and knows when to call a professional electrician. I would say that 90% of furnace and air conditioning equipment problems I have handled—that is, emergency service problems due to the equipment not operating—are of electrical origin. A good service technician must understand electricity.

If your heating air conditioning contractor does not understand how electricity works, how to size electrical wiring, or how to apply the safety codes required to supply power to your furnace and air conditioner properly, many different problems can occur. The new equipment could be damaged or have its life shortened; existing home appliances and devices that use electricity could be damaged or rendered useless; your house could catch fire and burn to the ground; in a worst-case situation, your contractor, you, or a family member could be killed instantly.

Again, I say, "Electricity is the only system in your home that can kill you instantly!"

Hire a professional!

ELECTRICITY FOR YOUR HVAC SYSTEM

The furnace is an appliance and is required to be on a dedicated circuit. The furnace circuit must be grounded. All furnace manufacturers require the furnace to be grounded. Grounding helps with the electronic component operations of the furnace as well as its safe operation. It is also required that a safety disconnect switch be located at the furnace and that the furnace be hardwired to that switch. Many heating and air conditioning contractors do not do this because many building departments do not enforce this code. They simply allow a cord to be used on the furnace so you can just plug it in to a receptacle. It is much safer for you and your air conditioning technician if a well-marked switch is used as a disconnect means rather than a cord. **Demand a safety disconnect switch!**

The condenser is also required to be on a dedicated circuit. This circuit is 220 volts and is a separate circuit from the furnace. The wires, fuses, and circuit breakers for the air conditioning condenser, which is located outside your home, should be sized for the maximum circuit ampacity, which is stated on the manufacturer's label glued to the condenser. *Not* the minimum circuit ampacity.

The fuses, which are located in the safety disconnect next to the condenser, are sized to protect your condenser. The circuit breaker in the electrical panel is used to protect the wiring, which feeds your condenser from the electrical panel, and the wiring needs to be sized large enough to handle the load of the air conditioning equipment. Sometimes, a non-fusible disconnect is used as a safety disconnect next to the condenser. If this is the case, the circuit breaker will also be used to protect the condenser.

I have come across many air conditioning installations, especially on new homes, where these items are sized for the minimum circuit ampacity of the condenser. If these items are not sized properly and are too small, your new multi-thousand-dollar investment will probably work acceptably, perhaps for a few years. But once there is a large heat load on the air conditioner or the condenser parts start to wear out a little, you may find the fuses blowing, the circuit breakers tripping, and the electrical components failing rather frequently. Improper wire, fuse, and circuit breaker sizing can also cause a fire, lead to premature part and equipment failure, and cost you more money.

A real headache and pain in the a … ah, *wallet.*

Chapter 8
The Control System

Control systems in furnace and air conditioning systems are beyond the scope of this book and are better left for the professional service technician. Here is a simplified explanation.

The thermostat, the control wiring inside the furnace, and the control wiring that goes between the furnace and the air conditioner are all 24 volts, low voltage. All other wiring, the wiring that feeds the equipment and the motors, is high voltage, 120 to 220 volts. Let a professional deal with the servicing of the equipment and keep your hands away from it. You will live longer.

The main control, the brain of the furnace, is the primary circuit board. The primary circuit board oversees the safe operation of the furnace and the blower. Furnaces also have many different built-in safety devices, high temperature limit switches, low limit temperature limit switches, high pressure and low pressure limit switches, blower door safety switches, and ignition verification switches are just a few of the safety controls that report back to the primary circuit board. These safety devices help protect the operation of the equipment, the welfare of your family, your home, and even the technician who performs the service.

Air conditioners vary in the type and number of controls inside the condenser. Basic 13 SEER models sometimes do not have any controls to protect the equipment. As you get up into the higher SEER or higher efficiency models of air conditioners with the better warranties, manufacturers install more controls for the protection of the equipment. I recommend the higher efficiency models for longer equipment life, fewer breakdowns, and lower operating costs, the benefits that add up to peace of mind!

THERMOSTATS

The only control that needs to concern a homeowner is the thermostat. The thermostat is simply a temperature-operated switch. If you want the temperature in your home to be 70⁰ in either heating or cooling mode, you simply turn the dial or set the temperature to 70⁰. When the room temperature in your home goes above or below 70⁰, a switch inside the thermostat closes and turns on your furnace or air conditioner.

When situating the thermostat, remember that the thermostat only responds to the air temperature at the exact spot where it is located. Thermostats should therefore be located close to the large return air grille because this is where the coldest air in your home will be in heating season and where the warmest air in will be in the cooling season. The thermostat should be at about chest height for the best comfort.

Thermostats come in a variety of makes and models and can control many aspects of the home comfort system, depending on the bells, whistles, and comfort additions you add to your home comfort system. Thermostats come in digital, non-digital, single stage, multiple stage, high visibility, programmable, and nonprogrammable, heat only, wireless, and high definition (HD). The newest wireless model even has a portable comfort device that you can take from room to room with you for ultimate comfort. I love technology!

The best thermostats for your comfort are the programmable models. Programmable thermostats allow you to set the temperature in your home according to your weekday and weekend schedule so that the furnace or air conditioner will turn on at a certain time of the day or night, at the temperature you want, up to four times in a twenty-four-hour period. You program the device according to your weekly schedule. Some programmable thermostats even allow you to program each day separately, according to your daily schedule. Models are even available that allow you to operate them from any computer or cell phone. The list of capabilities goes on and on.

Again, I love technology!

How nice is it to wake up on a cold winter morning and have your house be 70⁰ already. No more running to the thermostat, turning it on, and jumping back in bed until the house warms up. Or, in the other season, it's pleasant to come home on a 100⁰ day from your nice cool office, in your nice cool car, and walk into a nice cool home. You can do this without leaving your home comfort system running full blast all day and night. Awesome!

ZONING

Some homes have one furnace and air conditioner and two or more thermostats. This array is called zoning. Zoning thermostats, which are the same as other thermostats, talk to a control module that operates the furnace and air conditioner as well as the zone dampers, which are located in the ductwork. Zoning is nice if you have a large home, a two-story home, or the need to keep different parts of your house at different temperatures.

For example, if you have a two-story home, you probably notice that the upstairs is much warmer than the downstairs. If you had a zone control system, you could run your air conditioner and cool down the second floor without freezing out the first floor, and vice versa. On a cold winter day, you could keep the living areas of your home nice and warm all evening without heating the bedroom areas that are not being used.

Although zoning is an extremely nice feature to have and can keep you extremely comfortable, you need to be extra careful when choosing a contractor to install a zone system. There are additional controls that need to be installed to control the safety of your furnace and air conditioner as well as some additional ductwork, which needs to be installed to protect the home comfort system if only one zone is operating.

Unfortunately, zoning must be harder than I thought for some heating and air conditioning contractors. I have not been in one home in Northern California where the zoning has been installed properly by a builder. I have found that the additional ductwork and the added safety controls were missing in these installations. If you do not believe me, come to Sacramento—I will show you some residences that prove my point.

Do not let my warnings stop you from purchasing a zone control system; which is a great product. Just be careful about the contractor you choose to install it. And if you have zoning now, call a professional to inspect it for proper installation and safety controls. Adding the additional ductwork and safety controls can save you a lot of money in the future and help you enjoy the full benefits of your home comfort systems flexibility and comfort.

Chapter 9
The Exhaust System

The exhaust system helps keep you and your family alive. Attached to the heat exchanger in the furnace, it expels the combustion byproducts such as carbon monoxide, generated by the burning of fuel, to the exterior of your house. The exhaust system is very similar to a chimney that removes smoke when you burn wood in a fireplace. Without the exhaust system, we would not have furnaces to keep us warm and comfortable. Exhaust piping, sometimes called flue pipe, is made of double wall metal pipe for an 80% efficient furnace and can get extremely hot.

An exhaust system for a 90% or higher efficiency furnace is made of PVC. PVC is used because a lot of moisture, or condensate, is generated during the extra heat removal process that the 90% to 96% furnace goes through in the secondary heat exchanger. If metal pipe were used, it would rust, corrode, and fall apart. Due to the amount of heat added to the inside air by a 90% furnace, less heat is wasted, and the exhaust air is much cooler, so PVC rather than metal pipes can be used.

Exhaust system installations are among the key safety items that building inspectors look at during final inspection.

Chapter 10
The Duct System

The duct system is probably the most important subsystem within the home comfort system, but the duct system is also the most frequently misunderstood component. It truly amazes me that duct systems are still being designed and installed just as they were over fifty years ago. With all the advances in materials and technologies available today, there is no excuse for some of the ducting systems I have seen in homes and businesses.

The reason that most of you pay excessively to heat and cool your homes has much to do with faulty duct system design, faulty installation practices, and plain lack of care by the builders and installing contractors. These faulty designs are also big contributors to breakdowns and premature equipment failure. Duct systems are the veins of your home comfort system. They are attached to the furnace much like your arteries are attached to your heart, and they provide the pathways to get the warm and cold air distributed throughout your home.

We can measure the pressure of the duct system just as a doctor measures your blood pressure; we call the pressure within the duct system *static pressure*. All furnaces, with the exception of some variable speed blower models, are designed to operate at .5"of static pressure. If the static pressure in your duct system exceeds .5", you have a problem, just as if your blood pressure were too high. Too-high static pressure causes less airflow; it causes your furnace, air conditioner, and blower to work harder; it causes higher utility bills and premature equipment failure. High blood pressure causes less blood flow throughout your body, causes your heart and vital organs to work harder, and causes higher medical bills and premature death. What a coincidence.

A properly sized duct system is just as important, if not, more important, as a properly sized furnace and air conditioner. Cooling requires higher airflow than heating; 30%-50% more air moves through your duct system during cooling. As a result, you will need larger ducts so that your home comfort system can operate efficiently and with comfortable results.

Almost all homes I have worked on have ducts that were configured incorrectly and sized for heating only. These design practices have been carried over from a time when most homes did not have air conditioning. Old practices and habits, good or bad, pass from generation to generation like great-grandma's fruitcake recipe. These old-fashioned duct system designs are too small for air conditioning and have high static pressure. The air conditioning will still work, but it will cause problems.

Ducts that are too small restrict the airflow through the system, cause the furnace and air conditioner to work harder, and increase wear and tear on the equipment. This extra wear will cause more frequent breakdowns, shorten the life of your furnace and air conditioning equipment, and cause higher repair and operating costs. Smaller duct systems definitely cause your utility bills to go up because the equipment has to run longer and work harder to cool your home.

Remember one of the statistics mentioned in Chapter 2: According to the National Comfort Institute, the national average of furnace and air conditioning performance is just 57%.

If your system performs at that level, just over half the heating and cooling that your home comfort system produces is getting into the conditioned area of your home. Therefore, you are paying almost double, if not more, the amount it should cost you to heat and cool your home!

A properly sized duct system is the answer to this problem and a key element to obtaining the nametag efficiency rating of the furnace and air conditioner you purchase. Whether you replace the complete duct system or renovate your existing system, the results will be worth the price of the changes.

If you bought this book because you think you need a new furnace or air conditioner, and your current furnace and air conditioner is less than ten years old and does not heat and cool your home comfortably, call a properly trained and certified air diagnostics technician to test your duct system. You might only need duct renovation, which will save you thousands in new equipment costs and future utility bills.

The choice to renovate a ducting system does not mean that you need to replace all your ducts or that you need to buy a new furnace and air conditioner. It simply means optimizing the performance of the furnace and air conditioner in your home, making your house more comfortable, and saving you money.

To size ducts properly, a room-by-room load calculation should be performed by using a combination of Manual J and Manual D. Room by room load calculations are used to determine how much heating and cooling is needed to make the room comfortable, how much air is needed to get that amount of heating and cooling to the room, and how large the ducts need to be to get that air to the room.

The only way to prove that a system is performing up to its specifications is to test the operating performance of the work that was done. This testing is seldom performed on HVAC installations or service calls, even today. Look for a company that will guarantee you that the system you have purchased is operating at 90% or better of its rated capacity. The only way to prove this guarantee is to test and measure the system after it is installed. It may even be a good idea to hire another company, a third party, which is certified in air balancing and air diagnostics, to do the testing for you.

A key point to remember is that your local building department does not have the capacity or the knowledge to measure the performance of your home comfort system. They are simply supposed to make sure everything is installed safely and to code. California state law requires that the ducts be sealed so that there is less than 6% leakage. Duct sealing is not enough. In fact, you could even cause more damage to your furnace and air conditioner by causing them to work harder than they are designed for by reducing the amount of airflow the system is trying to produce. If you seal a duct system that is too small, you will still not get the air, the heating BTUs, or the cooling BTUs distributed throughout the home efficiently. It may even cost you more to heat and cool your home and cause you to use more energy (which everyone is trying to save). Certainly this practice will cause a whole array of other problems with your home comfort system, including premature failure.

Eventually, one can hope, the California Energy Commission will bring the whole picture together. They are working on it.

> Have you ever wondered why some rooms are too hot and some rooms are too cold?
> Have you ever wondered why your utility bill is too high?
> Have you ever wondered why some supply and return vents are loud and others are not?
> Have you ever wondered why your air conditioner never turns off?
> The number one answer to these questions is … ***the duct system!***

DUCT SYSTEM MATERIALS

Ducts come in different sizes, quality levels, material construction, and insulation value (R-Value). Many older homes have ducts that are made of round and rectangular sheet metal that comes in 3'- and 5' lengths. The insulation, if applied at all, is manually wrapped after the ducts are installed. Today we have a flexible duct product, which I like much better, called wire flex. Wire flex ducting comes in 25' and 50' lengths that can be cut to size. Using wire flex ducting, the contractor can assemble the duct system with fewer connections. A properly installed wire flex duct system is less likely to leak than sheet metal ducting. Standard wire flex ducting has an insulation R-value of 6.0 and is covered with a plastic outer shield, which can eventually deteriorate and fall off. I recommend using a wire flex duct with silver radiant barrier and a minimum R-value rating of 8.0. The radiant barrier also has a fiberglass mesh woven into the outer core to protect the duct integrity. All duct connections should be sealed with mastic to keep the air in the home out of the attic and crawl space and, prevent the dirty, dusty attic and crawl space air from moving into the living space.

Duct Type	Benefit
properly sized duct system	home is heated and cooled faster equipment operates at rated capacity equipment operates more efficiently equipment operates more quietly
insulation value R-6.0	standard R-value allowed by law
insulation value R-8.0 with radiant barrier	heat loss and gain is reduced through the walls of the duct utility bills are lower
radiant barrier	reflects attic heat away from duct helps keep conditioned air cooler/warmer within ducts outer coating of duct is more durable and will not fall apart ducts last longer utility bills are lower
duct sealing with silicone and mastic	keeps conditioned air inside the duct keeps attic and crawl area dust outside the home keeps home and ducts cleaner keeps ducts together keeps indoor air cleaner utility bills are lower

Chapter 11
Indoor Air Quality and Your Health

Indoor air quality is one hot topic today. With tighter-built homes, the off gassing chemicals used in products, mold, mildew, dirt, dust, pollens, allergens, and many other contaminants stay in the home and affect every breath we take. This is one reason that allergies and asthma are much more common today than ever before. Fortunately there is a way to help control these problems and make your home livable and comfortable.

AIR FILTRATION

Air filters were originally created to help keep equipment clean. They have evolved into devices to maintain indoor air quality, keeping the air we breathe clean. There are a variety of air filters on the market today, all intended to keep our indoor air clean. Some are known as horsehair, throwaway, pleated, electrostatic, electronic, and high efficiency particulate air (HEPA). To maintain good airflow and maintain the efficiency and comfort of your home comfort system, I recommend using a standard, inexpensive throwaway filter. These filters offer the least amount of restriction to airflow and will help protect your equipment.

If you are concerned with the indoor air quality of your home and would like to keep the air in your home extra clean by removing pollens and virus-sized contaminants from the air, I would recommend installing a separate HEPA filter to work in conjunction with your home comfort system. HEPA filter systems can be ducted in parallel to the return air duct system by removing a percentage of the return air from the duct system and returning clean, filtered air back to the return duct before it gets to the furnace blower.

Electronic Air Cleaners (EACs)

Electronic air cleaners assist in removing much more dirt (up to 99% of contaminants, according to some manufacturers) from the air than a standard air filter (up to 30% of contaminants but usually much less). Most EACs made by air conditioning manufacturers and sold by contractors are only rated to remove an average of 75% of the contaminants in the air, down to .5 micron. These will do a fair job. The better air cleaners are rated to remove up to 99% of all contaminants in the air, down to .3 microns. That means that such an air cleaner will even remove virus-sized particles.

I caution you on the use of electronic air cleaners. Sometimes two or three are needed, no matter what the manufacturer says, to maintain the proper airflow and efficiency of the home comfort system due to the amount of restriction created by the filter.

Electrostatic Air Filters

Electrostatic air filters are found in many homes and serve as a great add-on sale for those contractors willing to sell them. These devices, however, have their disadvantages. Most are very restrictive to the airflow of the home comfort system, are very hard to clean, and are not powerful enough to hold the smallest particles. They are not meant to be taken apart, though that is really the only way to clean them.

HEPA (High Efficiency Particulate Air) filters

HEPA filters are the best air filters on the market today and are rated to remove 99.97% of all contaminants, including pollens and virus-sized particles down to .3 micrometers in size. Think of the point on the tip of a very small needle. Hospitals and clean rooms in high tech firms use HEPA filters to keep sensitive areas clean. The core media in HEPA filters usually only has to be changed every five years.

ULTRAVIOLET (UV) LIGHTS

Ultraviolet lights have been used for years in water systems to kill bacteria. The UV light in duct systems does the same thing to bacteria in the air. As the air in your home comfort system passes by the UV light, mold, mildew, dust mites, viruses, bacteria, and many other biological contaminants are killed instantly. These are a must-have for people with allergies. When installed in a rated evaporator coil, one with a drain pan that is rated for UV use, they help keep the coil as clean as a whistle. UV filtration is also used in many hospitals for ultimate cleanliness and disinfection of the air and works fantastically well as a supplementary air cleaner in combination with a HEPA filter.

DUCT SEALING

Leaking ducts can decrease the overall efficiency of your furnace and air conditioner by 30% or more. The bigger the leak, the more your system efficiency decreases. Duct leaks not only affect the efficiency of your home comfort system; they also greatly decrease the comfort of your home. Sealing your properly sized ducts helps to keep the conditioned air, which you pay for, in your home. Sealing your ducts also helps keep your home cleaner by keeping the dirty and dusty attic, garage, and crawl space contaminants out of your home.

Do you realize that every time you turn on your furnace and air conditioner, you are sucking this contaminated air into your home through duct leaks?

You do now.

Do you see the black lines on your duct insulation above and below your furnace?

That's the air being sucked in and blown out through the leaks in your duct system. The insulation is acting as a filter as the hot and cold air passes through it. I guess it's okay if you want to heat and cool your garage, attic, and crawl space and don't mind a dusty home and larger utility bills. A quality-minded contractor who actually cares about your wallet, health, and safety will seal your furnace, air conditioner, and duct system using mastic and silicone. Most duct mastic is guaranteed for ten years, but with a proper seal, duct mastic should last forever and never fall off.

VARIABLE SPEED FURNACES

Variable speed furnaces, not multi-speed ones, are by far the #1 furnace choice to use when you are using indoor air quality products and are concerned about the cleanliness of the air you breathe. You can leave the extremely efficient ECM blower running twenty-four hours a day and 365 days a year, constantly cleaning the air you breathe throughout the whole house, not in just one room like the portable air filter products you buy at the department store. You don't even have to be heating or cooling the air. Just leave the fan switch located on the thermostat in the *on* position. The best part of this benefit is that it only costs as much as leaving a forty-watt light bulb turned on. That's 11.5 cents a day in a twenty-four-hour day at twelve cents per kilowatt. Not bad when it comes to your health.

ENERGY RECOVERY VENTILATORS (ERVs) AND HEAT RECOVERY VENTILATORS (HRVs)

Energy recovery and heat recovery ventilators bring fresh outside air into the home and exhaust stale indoor air to the exterior at the same time. The beauty of this add-on indoor air quality feature is that before the fresh outdoor air enters your home, it is filtered and preheated or precooled, depending on the season, using the temperature conditioned stale exhaust air that is being expelled from the home. HRV's and ERV's are a great way to control the fresh air ventilation in your home, especially if you have a tightly built house. HRVs are used in most areas around the country, and ERVs are mainly used in the south and other areas around the country where there is high humidity. You should check with your contractor to choose the proper recovery ventilator for your location and individual needs.

IAQ Product	Benefit
throwaway filters	keep equipment fairly clean inexpensive
electronic air cleaners	can remove 75% to 99% of all contaminants from the air in your home make the air your family breathes healthier makes the home healthier
electrostatic air filters	can removes small contaminants cleanable
HEPA filters	rated to remove 99.97% of all contaminants from the air in your home remove airborne bacteria remove airborne viruses make the air your family breathes healthier make the home healthier best air filters available
ultraviolet lights	kill airborne bacteria kill airborne viruses make the air your family breathes healthier and cleaner make the home healthier
duct sealing	keeps conditioned air inside the duct keeps attic and crawl area dust outside of the home keeps home and ducts cleaner keeps ducts together utility bills are lower keeps indoor air cleaner
variable speed furnaces	quietest furnace available most efficient blower motor best furnace to use with indoor air quality products extremely clean air inside the home when used in conjunction with electronic air cleaners, ultraviolet lights, and duct sealing
heat recovery and energy recovery ventilators	bring fresh air into the home exhaust stale indoor air from the home preheat/precool fresh air, using exhaust air for good efficiency

Chapter 12

Maintenance and the Maintenance Program Checklist

Maintenance of your heating and air conditioning system is required to keep the system clean and operating efficiently and safely. Maintenance can save you thousands of dollars over the life of your home comfort system.

Many people think that maintenance consists of changing the filter and that no more needs to be done. They could not be more wrong.

Maintenance allows the servicing company to keep the system running at peak performance and efficiency each year, locate worn parts in danger of failing during the next hot or cold spell, monitor the system performance, and perform a safety check to give you and your family peace of mind.

Manufacturers require that maintenance be performed at least once each year on the furnace and once each year on the air conditioner just to keep the warranties in good standing. For this reason alone, with part and compressor warranties extending up to ten years and heat exchanger warranties extending to twenty years or even the life of the furnace on high efficiency systems, maintenance should be performed strictly on schedule. One manufacturer even gives lifetime unit replacement warranties on the condenser, should the compressor or coil fail, and a lifetime furnace replacement if the heat exchanger fails. At least, the manufacturer does this if the buyer has done his/her part and had the system's maintenance care done on schedule. I would hate to see a client's face when a manufacturer denies a warranty claim for a heat exchanger or compressor due to the lack of proof of maintenance. That client would have to pay a couple of thousand dollars for the repair or just buy a new unit. Ouch!

A common misconception is that if a furnace and air conditioner are under warranty, the owner does not have to maintain the equipment. Warranty, however, does not equal maintenance! If a part fails and the manufacturer wants proof of maintenance before honoring the warranty and you don't have that proof of maintenance, do not blame the contractor. Just get out your checkbook.

The best way to keep your system maintained is to sign up for a maintenance program with a good service company that you trust, a service company that will show up at regularly scheduled times, usually every six months. They will become familiar with you and your equipment and most likely provide priority service and repair discounts due to your loyalty and continued relationship.

A good maintenance program should include the following key points.

- static pressure check in heating and cooling mode
- gas pressure check
- carbon monoxide check
- oxygen check
- tightening of electrical connections
- temperature rise measurement
- draft pressure measurement
- refrigerant pressures
- superheat or subcooling calculation to check refrigerant levels
- thermostat operation and calibration
- indoor coil inspection
- condenser coil (outdoor coil) cleaning
- evaporator coil inspection and cleaning (if accessible)
- condensate drain trap cleaning
- duct inspection
- filter inspection or cleaning
- priority service
- discounts on repairs

If your service company is not doing the inspections, cleanings, and readings listed above, start shopping for a new one.

One more thing!

Every time someone tests the performance of a car, a pump, an air handler or any machine or device, the output is checked and that item is tuned—except, unbelievably, furnaces. Even the manufacturers tell you that the inlet gas pressure should be adjusted to a certain value, depending on the type of fuel, and that's it.

The problem?

Gas pressure adjustment is the input variable of a gas furnace, not the output. If you really want a fine-tuned and efficiently operating furnace, find a company that tunes your furnace according to output—yes, the exhaust.

Chapter 13
Choosing the Right Contractor

The typical homeowner will only buy a home comfort system once in a lifetime. By now you should have a heightened understanding of furnaces, air conditioners, duct systems, and how they work together to form a comfortable and efficient home comfort system. You should also know what you hope to accomplish in your home and what is available for your comfort and efficiency. When you invite a contractor to your home to educate you on heating and air conditioning and give you your options for a new home comfort system, remember that it is usually not his fault that you need a new system and that you invited him as a guest into your home; he is there to help you.

However, how do you choose the right contractor?

Choosing the contractor for your home comfort system can be a daunting task. It requires a lot of time and research on your part, but I hope that I have made it a little easier for you.

Check with friends and neighbors for good recommendations about the good home comfort contractors they have used. Friends and neighbors are likely to tell you all you want to know, good and bad, about their experience with and knowledge of the contractors they have chosen in the past. You just have to ask.

Look for companies with additional certifications in air balancing, duct design, and combustion analysis from an organization like the National Comfort Institute.

Check the Internet or phone book for reputable companies operating in your area.

The phone book is a good source to find local contractors, but the Internet is indispensable. Not only can you find out who is operating in your area, you can also find out about other people's opinions and experiences with those companies, ratings from different sources about the company, and almost anything else you want to know that can help you make your decision.

Do research with the Better Business Bureau (BBB).

After you have chosen a few companies to interview, call the Better Business Bureau or go to their website and do a search on the contractors you have chosen to see if there have been any major complaints against them. The BBB rates all businesses and contractors in their system according to their documented history of complaints and complaint resolutions. This information can greatly affect your decision.

Check out the contractor with the contractors' licensing board for your state.

Call or go to your state contractors' licensing board (CSLB) website and do a search on the contractors you are thinking of inviting to your home and do some research on them. The CSLB will be able to give you license status, insurance information, personnel information, and a history of that information. The CSLB will also be able to tell you if there were any legal judgments against the contractor. This information will help you weed out the bad contractors. Some contractors are just bad—some unintentionally, some knowingly.

When it comes to hiring a good contractor, you want a true professional; you want someone you are comfortable with, someone you trust to do the best job for you.

Do not be afraid to ask a contractor who makes you uncomfortable to leave your home! They won't mind doing a bad job and taking your money.

I would stay away from people like the neighbor's brother-in-law who does HVAC for a living working for someone else but also does side work on the cheap.

The unlicensed and/or uninsured contractor is someone you should absolutely avoid, in any and all situations. If the person you hire is not licensed or insured, you are taking full responsibility for the job, your home, and that person's welfare. You will have no recourse, except in civil court, should something bad happen during the job. In other words, if the uninsured person you hire gets hurt, it's your responsibility, and you will be required to do things like pay millions of dollars because he cannot work for the rest of his life. If he burns your house down, your insurance company will not pay the claim because you hired an unlicensed, uninsured person. If this happens to you, hopefully you are independently wealthy or have a tent and enjoy camping in your backyard.

I would also advise you to stay away from large retail stores. If you choose to buy an air conditioner or any product from a department or hardware store, and that product needs to be installed by a contractor, you will not be able to choose the contractor who does the work in your home. You will be stuck with whoever does the work for that particular store—whoever the store sends to your home. The contractors they use may be good, but what happens if you do not like them? They are not store employees; they are subcontractors. Just as in the construction and remodeling industries, your general contractor subs out all the work he does not do to other contractors, or subcontractors. The problem with this is that you do not have a choice about the people they use or what types of equipment they use. In addition, if you do have a problem with the installation, whom do you call? The store or the contractor? Your guess is as good as mine. I'd say to call the store first, ask to speak with the manager who handles the installations and has accountability for results and customer complaints.

Heating, air conditioning, and home comfort systems are just too important to the comfort and safety of you, your family, and your home to let just anybody install them, and if they are not done right, they can cause aggravation for you and damage to your home. If you are using a general contractor to do a remodel or build a custom house, you should be the one working with your home comfort contractor and making the decisions about what you want done, how you want it done, and what options you desire. Nobody else should make those choices. You and your family are the people who have to live in the house. In addition, you should still pay the general contractor his markup, usually 15% to 20%, for the home comfort contractor's work, because the general contractor will still have to work with and coordinate the work with the home comfort contractor. Working with your general contractor and home comfort contractor in this way will give you peace of mind; you can feel sure that you are getting what you want from your home comfort system, and your general contractor will still be a happy camper.

Good heating and air conditioning contractors can be hard to find. Most are proud, hard-working, and technically knowledgeable. They have to be. As you have learned, the heating and air conditioning systems in your homes are made up of many complicated parts and systems. It takes years of training, education, and continued professional education each year to stay current on the new technologies and products that affect the work these professionals do. On top of all this, they have to become good business people too. Once you find a contractor who can put all this training and education together and understand all aspects of the business, maintain a relationship with that contractor and treat him with respect.

A good contractor will be licensed, insured, courteous, clean, professional, and understanding of your predicament. He will always present a written proposal outlining and detailing the proposed work and what he will be providing to you. Good contractors will talk about many of the things mentioned in this book and should ask many questions to find out about your needs and desires concerning a home comfort system. The good contractor will propose a variety of options, pricing, and payment options, including third-party financing, so you can purchase the best system that falls within your budget.

A great heating and air conditioning contractor will give you all the above plus a written performance guarantee for the system you have chosen.

The performance guarantee will assure you that the system you have purchased will operate at a minimum of 90% of what it is rated to produce. Not all contractors have the knowledge, training, experience, or capability to provide a performance guarantee.

Testing after installation is the only way that a system can be truly guaranteed. If the system is tested, a report will be generated with all the readings and explanations of those readings required to prove the system performance.

This report is your proof that you got what you paid for!

You should not have to ask for it, but make sure that you are given a copy of this performance report for your records along with a copy of your written agreement and a copy of your final building inspection.

Characteristics and actions of a good contractor

- clean
- courteous
- professional
- respectful
- organized
- measures the house and its attributes for a load calculation
- performs a load calculation
- gives you options for brands and equipment
- explains differences in brands and equipment
- explains system operation
- explains manufacturer warranties
- has written warranties and guarantees
- explains warranties and guarantees
- provides a performance guarantee for the system you have chosen
- provides written agreement
- explains written agreement
- provides payment options
- has a state contractor's license
- has proof of air diagnostics and duct design certification
- has proof of carbon monoxide and combustion analysis certification
- has proof of manufacturer and distributor training certifications
- provides proof of general liability insurance
- provides proof of Workmen's Compensation insurance
- provides city building permit
- explains the job process
- explains the amount of time they will be working in your home
- explains how your home will be protected
- provides proof that the employees working in your home have passed a criminal background check and a drug test

Characteristics and actions of a bad contractor

- does not have or prove any of the above to you
- looks at old equipment and tells you that you just need the same size
- gives you a price without performing a load calculation or giving you options
- does not have any warranties or guarantees
- does not have a performance guarantee
- is not licensed
- demands payment up front
- probably has the cheapest price
- tries to talk you out of a building permit or gives you an option to get one or not
- cannot prove insurances
- has a Better Business Bureau record of complaints
- makes you feel uncomfortable

Chapter 14
The Contract

The contract is your agreement between you and your contractor concerning the products you are purchasing, the work that the contractor will perform, and how much money you will be parting with for those products and services. Always get a complete contract with as much detail as possible. Get it in writing, get it before the work is started, and save it in a safe place. If you have a problem, miscommunication, or disagreement with your contractor, you will need the contract.

At a minimum, a good contract will be in writing and should include the following.

- names, addresses, and phone numbers of both parties
- contractor's license number
- contractor's insurance company information
- contractor's Workman's Compensation insurance company information if the contractor has employees
- contractor's bonding insurance company information
- description of the work being performed and all the work agreed to
- description of the major equipment being installed, including the manufacturer's brand and model number
- payment terms including a payment schedule if multiple payments are going to be made
- financing terms and payment schedule if the work is going to be financed
- start date of the work to be performed
- completion date of the work to be performed
- a list of warranties and guarantees and a written explanation of what they mean
- any state requirements, including special inclusions and language

All states have different requirements for home improvement contracts. These requirements can be found on your state's contractors state license board website or your state government's consumer information website. If you cannot find the requirements in the consumer section, look in the contractor section of the website, where there is plenty of information about what a contractor needs to supply to its customers when entering into contractual agreements with them.

Chapter 15

Preparing for Your Home Comfort System Purchase

You are already well on your way to being prepared for your home comfort purchase if you have purchased this book. Congratulations!

There are several other items about which I would like to touch base, and here they are.

1. Make sure your existing equipment is accessible to the contractors you will be interviewing so that they can get the information they need about them and take the measurements needed for the new equipment installation.
2. Clean off the kitchen table so you have a comfortable area to talk and review items discussed.
3. Try to have animals secured in another part of the house. I have been bitten more than once, even after I made friends with the animal.
4. Be ready to write a check for the down payment. Each state has different rules and regulations regarding down payments for construction work. Check with your state government to see what is acceptable by law.
5. Most importantly, since the choice of a contractor and a home comfort system is one of the most important decisions you will make as a homeowner, it is best if you and your significant other are present to speak with the contractor or the comfort consultant during the interview.

As you have learned by reading this book, there are many options available to you, and they affect your comfort, your health, and your safety. A tremendous amount of information is covered during a home comfort consultation, so it would be extremely hard for anyone to remember all the information and pass it on to a significant other. By having all of the decision makers present, the contractor can make sure that the needs and desires of each homeowner are being met and both persons' questions are being answered. In all probability, with all homeowners being present, it is likely that everyone involved will be happy at the end of the installation.

Chapter 16

Calculating Yearly Cooling Cost and Return on Investment

The yearly cooling cost of your air conditioner can be calculated with the following formula: BTUs/SEER=watts/1000=KW*rate*cooling hours.

BTU	= the British Thermal Units your condenser is rated for
SEER	= the seasonal energy efficiency rating your condenser is rated for
watt	= an electrical term used to define power
1000	= a divisor used to turn watts into kilowatts, which is how you are billed on your electric bill
kilowatt	= 1000 watts
rate	= the rate per kilowatt you pay on your electric bill
cooling hours	= the estimated hours you use your air conditioner each year per the US government. This varies by climate zone and is taken from a report generated by the US government. In the example, I use nine hundred hours. Nine hundred hours is the estimated run time of an air conditioning unit in the Sacramento and San Jose regions of California.

Example: An eighteen-year-old, three-ton air conditioner rated at 9 SEER, located in San Jose, California, where the client is paying seventeen cents per kilowatt for electricity, will cost $612.00 per year to operate.

BTUs/SEER=watts/1000=KW*rate*cooling hours
36,000/9 = 4000/1000 = 4 x .17 x 900 = $612.00.

If that client wanted to upgrade to a new 18 SEER unit, the yearly cooling cost would be $306 per year.

BTUs/SEER=watts/1000=KW*rate*cooling hours. 36,000/18= 2000/1000 = 2 x .17 x 900 = $306.00.

The upgrade would result in a yearly savings of $306.00 per year just for cooling.

RETURN ON INVESTMENT (ROI)

How long will it take to get my money back if I purchase a higher efficiency unit rather than a standard efficiency unit?

For example, if you currently have a five-ton air conditioner at 9 SEER, it costs you $1,020.00 per year to operate at seventeen cents per kilowatt. Upgrade to a 13 SEER, and your operating cost is $706. 00. Upgrade to an 18 SEER, and your operating cost is $510.00.

The yearly operating cost savings of upgrading to an 18 SEER air conditioner over a 13 SEER air conditioner amount up to $204 ($706-$510). If the 18 SEER unit cost an additional $3,000, then the return on investment would be $3000/$204 or 14.7 years.

BUT WAIT!

This may seem a long time to wait for a return on your investment. However, you also need to consider warranties on the new unit, repair costs that you will no longer pay now that you have the new unit, proper performance of the equipment you have purchased should you use a performance contractor, and increases in your electric rates, which average about 7% per year.

Just replacing your compressor on the old, inefficient unit will cost about $2,000, so if you figure just that into the calculation and do not consider anything else, your return on investment drops to 4.9 years.

$3000 (cost of upgrade)
less
$2000 (cost of repair)
equals $1,000 (true cost of upgrade instead of repair)
divided by

$204 (yearly operating cost savings)
equals
4.9 years time of return on investment.

Therefore, in just under five years, I will start putting at least $204 a year into my wallet because I purchased the higher efficiency equipment.

I will take that bet all day long.

In addition, just think, we didn't even consider the following items.

- the value of warranties on the new unit
- repair costs that the new unit will eliminate by replacing the old unit instead of repairing it
- increases in your electric rates, which average about 7% per year.
- proper performance of the equipment you have purchased. If you choose to hire a performance contractor and install a properly sized duct system(remember the national average of 57% performance) your existing cooling cost is most likely close to double what the above calculations show. Take this in to consideration along with the additional cost of a duct modification, and you will be putting at least $400 or more per year back in to your wallet after the payback period in the above example.

So how few years will payback really take?

Cooling Cost per Year Comparison
Based on 900 Hours per Year of Operation

(BTUs/SEER)=(watts)/1000=(kilowatts)*(rate)*900=yearly cooling cost

0.21   **per KW**

TONS	BTUs	SEER								
		4	6	9	10	12	13	14	16	18
3.0	36000	1701.00	1134.00	756.00	680.40	567.00	523.38	486.00	425.25	378.00
3.5	42000	1984.50	1323.00	882.00	793.80	661.50	610.62	567.00	496.13	441.00
4.0	48000	2268.00	1512.00	1008.00	907.20	756.00	697.85	648.00	567.00	504.00
5.0	60000	2835.00	1890.00	1260.00	1134.00	945.00	872.31	810.00	708.75	630.00

0.13   **per KW**

TONS	BTUs	4	6	9	10	12	13	14	16	18
3.0	36000	1053	702	468	421	351	324	301	263	234
3.5	42000	1229	819	546	491	410	378	351	307	273
4.0	48000	1404	936	624	562	468	432	401	351	312
5.0	60000	1755	1170	780	702	585	540	501	438	390

0.15   **per KW**

TONS	BTUs	4	6	9	10	12	13	14	16	18
3.0	36000	1215	810	540	486	405	374	347	304	270
3.5	42000	1418	945	630	567	473	436	405	354	315
4.0	48000	1620	1080	720	648	540	498	463	405	360
5.0	60000	2025	1350	900	810	675	623	579	506	450

0.17   **per KW**

TONS	BTUs	4	6	9	10	12	13	14	16	18
3.0	36000	1377	918	612	551	459	424	393	344	306
3.5	42000	1607	1071	714	643	536	494	459	401	357
4.0	48000	1836	1224	816	734	612	565	525	459	408
5.0	60000	2295	1530	1020	918	765	706	656	574	510

Chapter 17

Rules of Furnace and Air Conditioning Installation that Your Contractor, Sales Professional, or Boss Might Forget to Tell You

- **Rule #1** Always get a load calculation.
- **Rule #2** Always get a detailed proposal and agreement, in writing, before the work starts.
- **Rule #3** Always get a building permit.
- **Rule #4** Always meet the building inspector and get a signed permit upon job completion.
- **Rule #5** Always make the final payment to your contractor after the work is complete and the final inspection portion of the building permit is signed.

RULE #1
ALWAYS GET A LOAD CALCULATION.

Never replace a furnace or air conditioner without a proper Manual J load calculation. A load calculation determines the proper size of the equipment needed in the home. It is a measure of the heating and cooling needed to keep the conditioned space comfortable for the occupants. When I say *conditioned space,* I mean everything—the walls, floors, carpets, drapes, furniture, and air. A furnace or air conditioner that is too small will run too long, have unnecessary breakdowns, waste energy, waste money, and never heat or cool the home adequately when most needed—on the hottest or coldest day of the year.

A furnace and air conditioner that is too large will heat or cool the air in the home only and turn on and off too frequently. A system that is too large will run for short amounts of time, cool off the air only, and not absorb the heat from the walls, floors, furniture, etc. The heat inside these items will keep radiating to the air, warm the air up, and keep turning the air conditioner on for short periods of time. This will cause excessive wear and tear on the air conditioner components, which will cause them to fail faster. Each time the air conditioner starts up, it uses eight times or more power for short amounts of time, which keeps adding up, and costs you more money.

- Never accept anyone's guess about what size furnace or air conditioner you need.
- Never allow anyone to replace your furnace or air conditioner with one of the same size as the one you already have without first performing a load calculation.

Rule #2
Always get a detailed proposal and agreement.
In writing before the work starts.

It's the law. Anyone who does work for you in excess of $750 in California is legally obligated to provide a written agreement for that work, though the charge involved varies by state. Make sure the agreement you sign is the correct and current agreement approved by your state's Contractors State License Board. Check their website for a copy of all the correct elements for the project you are doing. Make sure you get the make and model number of the furnace and condenser at the time you sign the agreement. Then, should there be any changes to the job or the agreement with your contractor, make sure those changes are recorded in writing on a change order form and signed by both you and your contractor.

RULE #3
ALWAYS GET A BUILDING PERMIT.

A copy of the building permit must be posted at the job site at all times. The main function of a building permit is to have a city inspector look over the job and make sure that all items have been installed according to building codes and are safe to operate. Because he is able to provide a building permit, your contractor has proven to your local governing agency that he is licensed and insured.

RULE #4
ALWAYS MEET THE BUILDING INSPECTOR AND
GET A SIGNED PERMIT UPON JOB COMPLETION.

Even though there is a building permit for the work, that does not mean that the job has been inspected. Final inspection is the essential conclusive step. It is up to you or your contractor to call your governing agency that issued the building permit for final inspection. I recommend that you call for the final inspection and be present during that inspection.

RULE #5
ALWAYS MAKE THE FINAL PAYMENT TO YOUR CONTRACTOR AFTER THE WORK IS COMPLETE
AND THE FINAL INSPECTION PORTION OF THE BUILDING PERMIT IS SIGNED.

The final inspection is the contractor's final requirement when installing home comfort equipment. By the time of the final inspection, all the equipment should be installed and operating, all the performance reports should be complete, all the third party inspections should be complete, and the work area should be clean. Once the final inspection is complete and the building permit has been signed, pay your contractor. He has worked hard to gain your trust and keep you happy, and payment for a job well done is how you will keep him happy. The final payment should be at least 10% of the job; otherwise, you paid your contractor too much too soon.

Chapter 18
The End

There you have it! I truly hope that you have been enlightened, educated, and informed so that you are confident and comfortable enough to make a proper decision when you purchase your home comfort system and the right choice of your contractor, who will then be your newest friend.

And here's to your health, to your safety, and to your comfort!